WORLDVIEWS

A CHILDREN'S INTRODUCTION TO MISSIONS

Written by Sarah Lewis

Published by Pioneers
10123 William Carey Dr
Orlando, FL 32832 U.S.A

ISBN 978-0-9899545-6-3

The Team: Matt Green, Nathan Burns, Joseph Boyle, Daniel Anan, Tim Twinem, Ben Johnson.
Illustrations by Ronald Rabideau, www.ronaldrabideau.com
Videos & Design by Parable Media, www.parable.media

Printed in the United States of America

First Edition 2017

THIS IS GOD'S STORY

In the beginning God created the heavens and the earth. Before there was time, or air, or water, God had a great idea...

He formed our world, and He made it beautiful—full of sounds and colors and smells and tastes. He created animals and plants and stars and everything on the earth and in the sky. And then, as His last and most wonderful creation, He made people. Do you know what was so special about people? What made them different from everything else He made? God created people in His image—to be like Him and to know Him. God put a special desire in people's hearts to worship Him. And all of creation shows how worthy God is to be praised.

A worldview is the way that a person looks at the world. It's what a person believes about who they are, where they came from, and why they are here. A person's worldview is shaped by many things: where they live, what the people around them believe, what experiences they have, and what things they care most about.

If you are a follower of God and use the Bible to determine who you are, where you came from, and what you are here for, then you have a Biblical Worldview. Through this study we will learn about five other major worldviews and the people that represent them.

To help us remember the worldviews we are studying, we will use an acronym called THUMB. That stands for Tribal, Hindu, Unreligious, Muslim, and Buddhist.

Okay, so hold out your thumb. Look very closely at it. What do you notice? Can you see your fingerprint? Did you know that every person has a unique fingerprint? No two thumbs are the same. As we learn about people from all over the world, remember that they are uniquely special to God. He made every single person and no two people are the same! God wants everyone to know how special they are to Him. No matter who they are or where they come from, anyone can be a part of His story.

WHAT IS A WORLDVIEW?

WHAT IS "T-H-U-M-B"?

You may know that the story didn't end there. God had an enemy who wanted to destroy all that God had made. His name was Satan, and his goal was to ruin God's relationship with people. It didn't take long before his plan seemed to be working. The very first people God created forgot why they were created and they even started to forget how good it was to know God. They believed a lie from Satan instead of God's truth, and they turned away from God. But God already had a plan to restore His relationship with people. He promised that one day He would defeat Satan once and for all and rescue His people from all of their forgetting. They would remember why they were created, and they would remember how good it was to know and love Him.

Do you know how God would do it? It might sound like a strange plan, but God would rescue His people by sending His Son to die for them. Jesus came down from heaven and entered earth as a person. He showed people how to worship God. And then He gave His life as a way to pay for all the mistakes people had made. He died on a cross and made a way for people to be restored to God.

THIS IS A TRUE STORY

This is a true story. There are many more details, but this true story is called the gospel. Some people hear it, believe it, and follow God. Some people hear it, reject it, and follow Satan. And some people have never heard it. If you are a follower of God then one of the most important jobs you have on earth is to share the gospel; to tell people the story of God and the great lengths He has gone to help them know Him and love Him. That's why in this study we are going to be talking about people all over the world who don't know the story (or don't believe the story) of God. We will learn about who they are, where they live, the different things they believe, and how we can share the gospel with them.

TRIBAL

The first worldview we will look at is the *Tribal* worldview. Can you unscramble these Tribal words and match them to their explanations?

Tribal people believe that objects around them have **SPIRITS** inside them.

Sometimes Tribal people worship their family members who lived before them. They are called **ANCESTORS**.

Believing that spirits control things is called **ANIMISM**.

Tribal people are very **AFRAID** of these spirits.

Most Tribal people use **STORY TELLING** as a way to teach what they believe.

INSIMMA

AARIFD

TSIIPRS

SCNEOTRSA

YROST LLENGIT

GENEROUS JARS

MAKE A GENEROUS JAR AND HELP RAISE MONEY FOR THE TARAHUMARA!

This week we will be learning about a special group of people with a Tribal worldview. They are the Tarahumara people of Mexico. You will watch a video about them, learn interesting things about their culture, and even try some of their food! As you learn about them, you will also be raising money to help them. To get started we are going to create a generous jar. Here's how:

1. Find an empty jar in your house. You might have to ask an adult for help. It could be a tin can (make sure the edges aren't sharp) or an old spaghetti sauce jar. Once you've decided on a jar, make sure it's clean and dry.

2. Find your THUMB sticker and put it on your jar. Fill out the word TRIBAL next to the "T."

3. Begin filling your jar!

TRIBA

WHERE IN THE WORLD ARE

L PEOPLE?

DRAW A LINE TO THE MATCHING COUNTRIES ON THE MAP WHERE TRIBAL PEOPLE CAN BE FOUND:

Mexico   Ethiopia   Nigeria   Brazil   Papua New Guinea   Peru

DAY TWO

DO CHRISTIANS AND TRIBAL PEOPLE HAVE THE SAME

WORLDVIEW?

Cut out each box on the dotted lines. Then read the sentence in each box. If it is something a Tribal person believes, paste it into the TRIBAL column. If it is something the Bible teaches, paste it into the BIBLE column.

TRIBAL

BIBLE

When I do something wrong I can be forgiven through Jesus.

Bad things and good things happen in my life because God has a plan for me.

If I have done something wrong I need to do special things to make spirits happy again.

There are demons and angels in this world, but I should not be afraid because God is in control.

When I die I will become a spirit that lives inside an animal or plant.

Many animals and plants have spirits inside them. I should be afraid of them because they are powerful.

If bad things happen in my life, it is because I did something wrong and a spirit is mad at me.

When I die I will go to heaven or hell.

TRIBAL
BIBLE VERSE

Most Tribal people are afraid of spirits. The enemy of God wants Tribal people to stay afraid and never be happy or free. But Jesus came to rescue them from spirits and give them a new and better life in Him. Color this Bible verse and think about How God might want to use you to show His love to Tribal people.

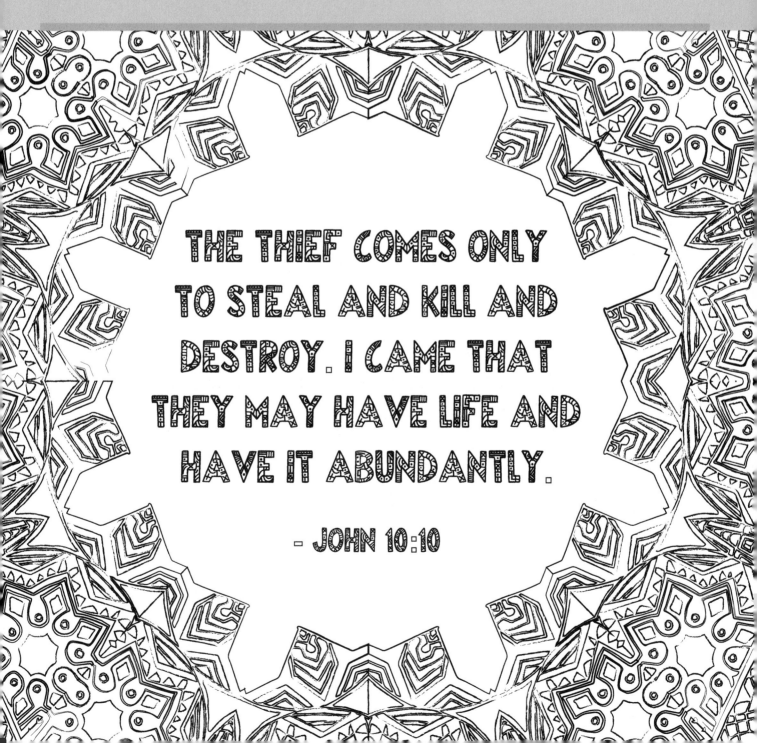

THE THIEF COMES ONLY TO STEAL AND KILL AND DESTROY. I CAME THAT THEY MAY HAVE LIFE AND HAVE IT ABUNDANTLY.

- JOHN 10:10

THE
CULTURE

Did you know that the Tarahumara people have different houses, clothes, and even food, than we do here in America? Here are some interesting facts about their culture:

Tarahumara people live in the deserts of Mexico. Most of the land has high cliffs and can be pretty tricky to walk around.

Their homes are made of adobe, which is a type of mud that hardens and becomes very strong.

It's very dry in the desert. There are only a few types of plants that can grow. If you're ever visiting Copper Canyon, watch out for cacti.

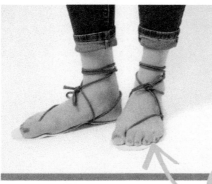

Tarahumara women love to wear brightly colored dresses that help them stand out in the brown desert.

The Tarahumara people are good runners. They run for a very long time without needing to stop. They run wearing special sandals they call *huaraches*.

SHARING
GOD'S STORY

How would you tell a Tribal person about Jesus?

In many Tribal cultures people tell stories instead of reading books. They can remember very long stories and tell them over and over again.

Can you think of a Bible story to tell a Tribal person? What story might be special for them to hear?

Turn your Bible story into a picture book and practice telling it to a friend or parent.

Who knows, maybe someday you can use your picture book to tell a Tribal person about Jesus.

Can you think of a story that would help a Tribal person see that God is more powerful than spirits?

Kobisi Energy Bars

ingredients

1 cup cornmeal
2/3 cup water
3 tablespoons agave
2 tablespoons chia seeds
a dash of cinnamon

directions

Step One:
Preheat the oven to 350ºF.

Step Two:
Toast the cornmeal in a pan on medium heat until it becomes slightly brown (about 5 minutes).

Step Three:
Add all the ingredients to a food processor and pulse until there are no large chunks remaining. If the mixture is too crumbly, add a little more water until you're left with a thick paste.

Step Four:
Form the mixture into small bars. Bake on a nonstick tray for about 10-12 minutes until the outside forms a solid crust and begins to show small cracks. Remove from the oven, let cool, and enjoy!

EAT LIKE THE
TARAHUMARA

Many of the foods that the Tarahumara people eat are made from the plants and vegetables they can grow on their land. One of the main foods they eat is called kobisi.

To make kobisi, corn kernels are taken off of the cob. Then the corn is roasted over a fire until it is browned (sometimes it even pops into popcorn). After it has cooled, the corn is ground between two stones until it turns into a powder. Spices are added to help flavor the powder, and the kobisi is ready to be used.

Want to give it a try? Follow the recipe above to see if you enjoy eating like the Tarahumara.

WEAVE LIKE THE
TARAHUMARA

Baskets are woven from leaves of the sotol plant.

The Tarahumara people live far away from cities. When they need something they can't go to the store to buy it, so often times they make it themselves.

One way they make things is by weaving. The Tarahumara are very good weavers and can make things like bowls, plates, and even blankets out of materials they find nearby.

WANT TO GIVE IT A TRY?
With the help of a grown up, follow the steps on the next page to weave your own bowl.

YOU'LL NEED:
- 1 pair of scissors
- 1 paper plate
- a few different colors of yarn
- 1 hole punch
- 1 pen or pencil

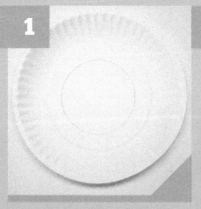

1

Trace a circle in the middle of your plate. Be sure to make it as centered as you can.

2

Cut 11 straight lines from the edge of the plate to the edge of the circle. Make sure the slits are evenly spaced.

3

Widen each slit so that it is about 1/2 inch wide and comes to a point in the center.

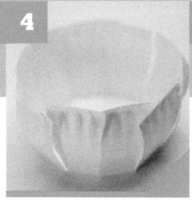

4

Fold the tabs into the center creating a circle where you first traced it.

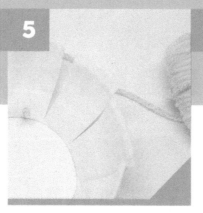

5

Poke a small hole in the bottom of one tab. Thread a piece of yarn through the hole and tie a knot at the end of the yarn.

6

Weave the yarn around the plate by going inside and outside of each tab. Continue until you are almost to the top of the plate.

7

Using a hole punch, make two holes near the top edges of each tab.

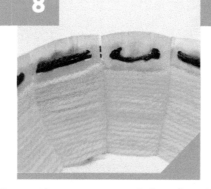

8

Weave the yarn around the plate by going inside and outside of each hole. Continue until you have gone around the whole plate.

9

Tie off the yarn and knot it several times. Cut off any extra yarn. Enjoy your basket!

HINDU

The second worldview we will look at is the *Hindu* worldview. Can you match these Hindu words to the clues to complete the crossword puzzle?

KARMA

MANY LIVES

REINCARNATION

BRAHMAN

MANY GODS

DHARMA

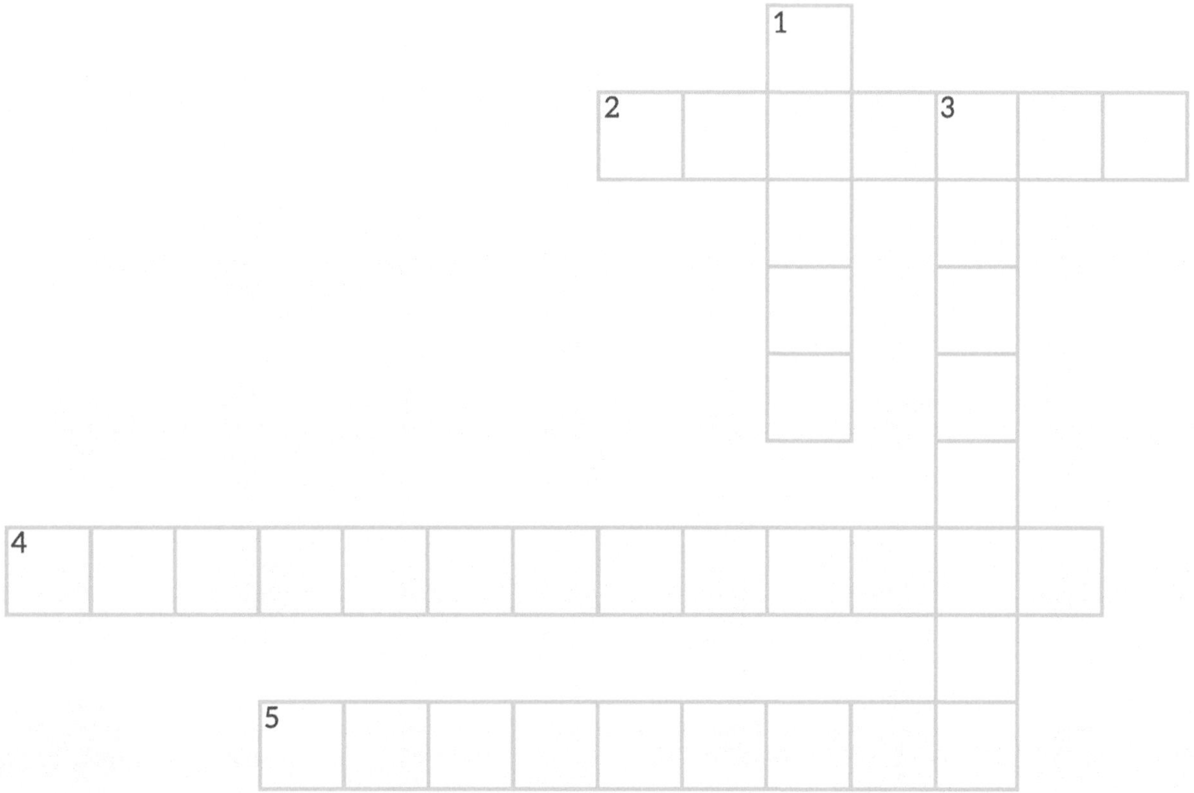

Down:

1. _______ means that when you make good choices, good things will happen to you. When you make bad choices, bad things will happen to you.

3. Hindu people believe that there are _______ _______.

Across:

2. They believe that there is one god who is the most powerful. He is called _______.

4. Hindus believe that when a person dies they come back to life as another person. This is called _______.

5. Because of reincarnation, a Hindu believes they will live _______ _______ on earth.

SEE THE SCALE THAT SAYS "DHARMA?" HINDUS BELIEVE THAT LIVING WELL CAN MAKE THE WORLD BALANCED JUST LIKE THAT SCALE.

GENEROUS JARS

MAKE A GENEROUS JAR AND HELP RAISE MONEY FOR THE PEOPLE OF INDIA!

Throughout this week we will learn about a particular group of people with a Hindu worldview. They are a group of women and children from India. You will watch a video about them, learn interesting things about their culture, and even try some of their food! As we learn about them, we will be raising money to help them. To get started we are going to create a generous jar. Here's how:

1 Grab your generous jar.

2 Fill out the word **HINDU** next to the "H."

3 Begin filling your jar!

HIND

WHERE IN THE WORLD ARE

U PEOPLE?

DRAW A LINE TO THE MATCHING COUNTRIES ON THE MAP WHERE HINDU PEOPLE CAN BE FOUND:

India   Nepal   Sri Lanka   Bangladesh   Bhutan   Pakistan

DO CHRISTIANS AND HINDU PEOPLE HAVE THE SAME

WORLDVIEW?

Cut out each box on the dotted lines. Then read the sentence in each box. If it is something a Hindu person believes, paste it into the Hindu column. If it is something the Bible teaches, paste it into the Bible column.

HINDU

BIBLE

When I make good choices, good things will happen in my life. When I make bad choices, bad things will happen in my life.

Jesus is the only way to God.

There isn't only one right path to God. Everyone can make up their own path.

There is only one God.

When I die I will start a new life on earth as a different person or animal.

When I make bad choices in my life, I need to ask Jesus to forgive me.

There are many, many different gods.

When I die I will go to heaven or hell.

HINDU
BIBLE VERSE

Do you know what the word weary means? It means to be tired or worn out from working very hard. Hindu people work very hard to make good choices. They believe that if they make too many bad choices, they will have to come back to earth after they die and try all over again. And again, and again, and again....until they can live a perfect life. For many Hindu people, this can cause weariness.

Jesus wants Hindus to know that they can be forgiven for their bad choices. They don't have to try to be perfect because Jesus was perfect for them. As you color this verse, think of how tiring life is for a Hindu person, and think about how Jesus wants them to find rest in Him. Ask God how He wants to use you to share His message of rest with a Hindu person.

come to me, all who are weary and heavy-laden, and i will give you rest.

-matthew 11:28

THE CULTURE

India is a very different place than America. Read about how people live in India and imagine what it would be like to grow up in their culture.

India is a country with over a billion people living in it. Because it is crowded, most people ride in little vehicles called rickshaws to get around.

India has many beautiful buildings. One of the most famous buildings in India is called the Taj Mahal.

Women wear beautiful dresses called saris. Saris are made from one long piece of fabric that is wrapped around the waist and then draped over one shoulder.

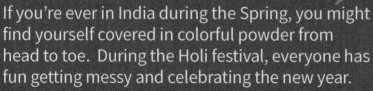

India has many colorfully painted statues called idols. These idols are often given food or gifts as a way to worship them.

If you're ever in India during the Spring, you might find yourself covered in colorful powder from head to toe. During the Holi festival, everyone has fun getting messy and celebrating the new year.

SHARING
GOD'S STORY

How would you tell a Hindu about Jesus?

In India, there is a special art called Henna. Women draw symbols on their hands that can tell a story. Did you know you can use henna to tell a Hindu person about Jesus?

Read The story of the Prodigal Son (Luke 15:11-32). What kinds of symbols could you draw to show what happens in the story? Use the hand on this page to draw your symbols and practice telling the story.

If you happen to make a Hindu friend, talk to him or her about the Prodigal Son and God's forgiveness. Better yet, invite them over and tell the story as you do henna together.

Paratha

ingredients

2 cups whole wheat flour
1-2 teaspoons oil
1/2 teaspoon salt
water
splash of oil (for roasting)

directions

Step One:
In a bowl mix the flour, salt, oil, and a splash of water. Knead into a ball of dough, adding more water as needed. Cover and set aside for 30 minutes.

Step Two:
Pinch a medium sized ball from the dough and dust with flour. Flatten to about a 4-inch diameter with a rolling pin.

Step Three:
Spread a bit of oil on the surface of the dough and then fold in half. Repeat once more.

Step Four:
Dust again with flour and use the rolling pin to flatten to a circle about 7 inches in diameter.

Step Five:
Sauté in a skillet over medium heat until lightly golden on each side. Serve warm.

EAT LIKE THE
PEOPLE OF INDIA

Indian food has many spices such as chili pepper, black mustard, coriander, cardamom, turmeric, ginger, and cumin. Many of these spices are very colorful and can even be used as dye. So if you every go to India, expect a lot of color and a lot of flavor!

In India, there is a popular flat bread called paratha. Paratha is usually dipped into a sauce made from all those colorful spices.

Want to give it a try? Follow the recipe above to see if you enjoy eating like the people of India.

SEW LIKE THE
PEOPLE OF INDIA

India is full of many bright and beautiful fabrics. These fabrics are used to make everything from traditional clothing, to purses, pillows, and even shoes.

Some fabric-related words that we use in English actually came from India, like *gingham*, *calico*, and *khaki*.

The cotton fabrics are made from cotton plants grown on farms. Silk is made from wild silk moths. Wool is made from the fleece of goats that live in the mountains.

The India HIV project uses these fabrics to give women a job. The women make colorful purses and stuffed animals, and then they sell them all over the world.

WANT TO GIVE IT A TRY?
Follow the instructions to make your own fabric

YOU'LL NEED:
- 1 pair of scissors
- 2 sheets of craft paper
- string
- 1 hole punch
- tape
- a handful of cotton balls

1

Draw an outline of an animal on one piece of paper. It works best if you make your outline as big as possible.

2

Stack both of your pieces of paper together and cut around the outline.

3

Using bright colors, make patterns and designs on each side of your animal cutout to make it look like fabric.

4

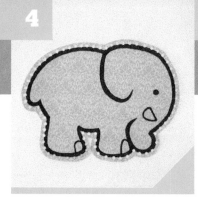

With the papers stacked together, punch holes along the edge of the shape.

5

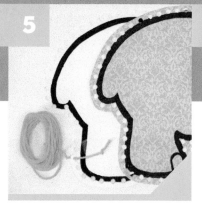

Tie a knot on the end of your string. Tape your string on the inside of one piece of paper so that it doesn't show when the papers are stacked.

6

Pull your string up through the hole closest to where you taped it, then put your two pieces of paper back together.

7

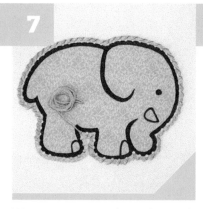

Weave your string through the holes around the outside of your paper. Leave about two inches unsewn.

8

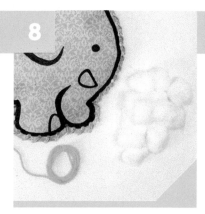

Stuff your cotton balls into the middle of the paper through your hole. Make sure not to rip your paper.

9

Finish weaving the string to close the hole. Tie the remaining string to the string it meets with back at the beginning. Give it a name!

UNRELIGIOUS

The third worldview we will look at is the *Unreligious* worldview. After reading the sentences below, see if you can find the bold words in the word search.

Most unreligious people believe that the earth has no **CREATOR**. They do not believe that there is a God. That is called **ATHEISM**. Atheism means **WITHOUT GOD**.

Many unreligious people believe that everything can be explained through **SCIENCE** because everything is **NATURAL**. There is nothing **SUPERNATURAL** about the earth or the people in it.

Unreligious people believe that **HUMANS** are **GOOD** and can decide what is **RIGHT** and **WRONG** without God.

Most unreligious people believe that a person stops **EXISTING** after they die because there is no **SPIRITUAL** part of a person.

```
S S D L S C I E N C E L X N Q
C U H C T Y I K X A Y A M A E
Q Z P S C W G Z Y P J W R N E
J S B E G R I O J O V Z C I X
B W P B R W E T Y W T R U F I
D V L I U N R A H L A W S E S
P A H J R X A O T O P O W S T
G D T L E I G T N O U Y E M I
O K J H E O T R U G R T S K N
O H E C E R X U I R L U G G G
D U Q C K I D S A G A I Y O G
I M E T B G S Q J L H L K L D
Z A T B W P C M H N E T C T J
M N F T N A T U R A L N K M P
F S L U O Y F R I F V D C B J
```

supernatural	without god	spiritual
athiesm	creator	natural
wrong	science	right
existing	humans	good

GENEROUS JARS

MAKE A GENEROUS JAR AND HELP RAISE MONEY FOR HUNGARIANS!

Throughout this week we will learn about a particular group of people with an Unreligious worldview. They live in a country called Hungary. You will watch a video about them, learn interesting things about their culture, and even try some of their food! As we learn about them, we will be raising money to help them. To get started we are going to create a generous jar. Here's how:

1 Grab your generous jar.

2 Fill out the word **UNRELIGIOUS** next to the "**U.**"

3 Begin filling your jar!

UNRELIG

WHERE IN THE WORLD ARE
[REL]IGIOUS PEOPLE?

 Ireland Germany France Italy Hungary China

DO CHRISTIANS AND UNRELIGIOUS PEOPLE HAVE THE SAME

WORLDVIEW?

Cut out each box on the dotted lines. Then read the sentence in each box. If it is something an Unreligious person believes, paste it into the Unreligious column. If it is something the Bible teaches, paste it into the Bible column.

UNRELIGIOUS

BIBLE

When I die, I stop existing. There is nothing after death.

God wants all people to know Him and to love Him.

The universe was not created.

I can make up my own ideas about what it right and what is wrong.

God made everything that exists.

God is probably not real, and if He is, He does not want us to know Him.

God gave us His laws as a way for us to know right from wrong.

I was made with a soul. I am going to live forever in heaven or in hell.

UNRELIGIOUS
BIBLE VERSE

Many Unreligious people believe only in the things that they can see and explain. For them, life on earth is the only time to find happiness. They don't believe that there is anything beyond life on earth so their experiences here are the best they will ever have.

God made us to experience wonderful things after life on earth. For those who love God, the very best things are waiting for them in Heaven. He is preparing things that we can't even imagine. God wants Unreligious people to love Him and to experience Heaven. As you color this page and read this verse, think about people who don't have hope after this life. Pray that God would give them eyes to see beyond this world and hope for a life in Heaven with Him.

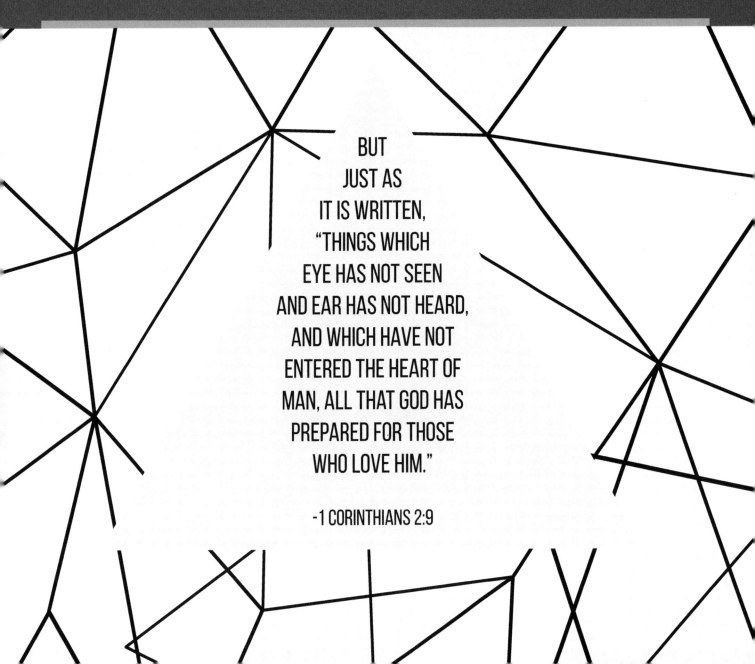

BUT JUST AS IT IS WRITTEN, "THINGS WHICH EYE HAS NOT SEEN AND EAR HAS NOT HEARD, AND WHICH HAVE NOT ENTERED THE HEART OF MAN, ALL THAT GOD HAS PREPARED FOR THOSE WHO LOVE HIM."

-1 CORINTHIANS 2:9

THE CULTURE

Have you ever thought about living in Hungary? Read about the Hungarian lifestyle and imagine what it would be like to live in their culture.

Hungarian homes are made out of clay. The clay is made into thick walls that help keep the home warm in the winter and cool in the summer.

In Hungary, people decorate eggs using a special wax pen and dye made from vegetable peels.

Hungary has many forms of art, but they are best known for their embroidery. They use colorful thread and make decorations on fabrics of all kinds.

It might seem strange to see so many churches in an Unreligious culture, but Hungary wasn't always Unreligious. Most Hungarians were Christians hundreds of years ago.

Hungarian clothing is very vibrant and detailed. Women wear dresses with carefully embroidered patterns that are often stitched by hand.

SHARING GOD'S STORY

How would you tell an Unreligious person about Jesus?

Did you know that in Unreligious cultures, being nice is a very important way to share Jesus with someone?

If you can be a happy and kind friend, many times people will ask what makes you so happy and kind. You can tell them about how following Jesus teaches you to be kind to others. You can also tell them about how being forgiven by Jesus has made you happy.

Can you think of a way to show kindness to someone? Draw a picture of what you might do to be a good friend.

Körözött

ingredients

1 cup cottage cheese
1 finely chopped red onion
1/3 cup butter
1 heaping tablespoon sour cream
1 teaspoon ground paprika
1/2 teaspoon salt
1/2 teaspoon ground caraway seeds

directions

Step One:
In a small bowl blend cottage cheese with butter and sour cream.

Step Two:
Mix in all other ingredients.

Step Three:
Chill in fridge for 2-3 hours.

Step Four:
Serve with fresh bread.

EAT LIKE THE
HUGARIANS

Have you ever had fresh vegetables picked from a garden? In Hungary, many people eat what they get from farms. They even get their cheese from sheep farmers.

One of the things people eat the most in Hungary is called paprika. It is a bright red spice that is used in many meals. One appetizer combines their love of cheese and their love of paprika into a creamy dip called körözött.

Want to give it a try? Follow the recipe above to see if you enjoy eating like the Hungarians.

BUILD LIKE
HUNGARIANS

Hungary has many castles. Most of them are hundreds of years old. Castles have many different features. Each part is made for a special reason.

Early castles were made out of wood and dirt. Later people began making them with stone.

WANT TO GIVE IT A TRY?
Gather your supplies and see how many different features you can include in your own castle.

YOU'LL NEED:
- recycling scraps from around the house such as toilet paper rolls, cereal boxes, plastic bottles, paper plates, etc.
- 1 pair of scissors
- glue or tape
- markers of crayons

THE MOAT

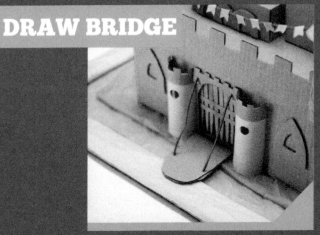

A moat is a ditch that is dug out around the castle and then filled in with water. This makes it hard for people to attack because they have to get through the moat to get to the castle.

DRAW BRIDGE

If your castle has a moat then you also need a draw bridge. A draw bridge is a large wooden bridge that can be lowered to let people cross the moat. It is raised when the castle is under attack.

TOWERS

Towers are tall, round structures built around the curtain wall. They help the guards see the attackers below.

CURTAIN WALL

The curtain wall is a large wall that protects the castle. The top usually has openings where guards could shoot arrows or drop stones.

PORTCULLIS

The front door of the castle is thick and hard to break through. In front of it is a spiky iron gate called a portcullis.

LOOPS

Arrow loops are small slits in the castle walls where archers could shoot an arrow without being exposed. They are usually shaped like a cross.

MUSLIM

The fourth worldview we will look at is the *Muslim* worldview. Can you match these Muslim words to the clues and discover the secret word?

JUDGEMENT

ISLAM

QURAN

PARADISE

FIVE PILLARS

EARN

MUHAMMAD

1. ☐ ☐ ☐ ☐

2. ☐ ☐ ☐ ☐ ☐ ☐ ☐ ☐ ☐ ☐ ☐

3. ☐ ☐ ☐ ☐ ☐ ☐ ☐ ☐

4. ☐ ☐ ☐ ☐ ☐ ☐ ☐ ☐

5. ☐ ☐ ☐ ☐ ☐ ☐ ☐ ☐ ☐

6. ☐ ☐ ☐ ☐ ☐

7. ☐ ☐ ☐ ☐ ☐

1. Muslims do many things to _____ favor with Allah.

2. There are five main things Muslims must do to follow Allah. They are known as the _____ _____ .

3. The religion of Islam was started by a man named _____ .

4. If a person has done enough to earn favor with Allah, they will be in _____ after they die.

5. Everyone will face _____ based on their choices.

6. Followers of Allah are part of a religion known as _____ .

7. Muhammad wrote a book that is called the _____ .

MUSLIMS CELEBRATE A HOLY MONTH. LOOK AT THE LETTERS IN THE RED SQUARES TO SEE WHAT IT IS CALLED. WRITE IT HERE: _____

GENEROUS
JARS

MAKE A GENEROUS JAR AND HELP RAISE MONEY FOR REFUGEES!

Throughout this week we will learn about a particular group of people with a Muslim worldview. They are refugees from Iraq and Syria. You will watch a video about them, learn interesting things about their culture, and even try some of their food! As we learn about them, we will be raising money to help them. To get started we are going to create a generous jar. Here's how:

1 Grab your generous jar.

2 Fill out the word **MUSLIM** next to the "**M**."

3 Begin filling your jar!

MUSL

WHERE IN THE WORLD ARE
M PEOPLE?

DRAW A LINE TO THE MATCHING COUNTRIES ON THE MAP WHERE MUSLIM PEOPLE CAN BE FOUND:

Iraq   Syria   Indonesia   Chad   Turkey   Afghanistan

DO CHRISTIANS AND MUSLIM PEOPLE HAVE THE SAME

WORLDVIEW?

Cut out each box on the dotted lines. Then read the sentence in each box. If it is something a Muslim person believes, paste it into the Muslim column. If it is something the Bible teaches, paste it into the Bible column.

MUSLIM

BIBLE

I can be sure that I am saved because I have believed in Jesus and repented of my sin.

There is nothing I can do to make myself pure.

There are many important things I need to do to keep myself pure.

God spoke his perfect message through the prophet Muhammad.

God created people in His image.

No one can know if they are saved until Judgement Day.

God speaks His perfect message through Jesus, and through the Holy Spirit.

God created everything completely different from Himself. Nothing He made is like Him in any way.

MUSLIM
BIBLE VERSE

Muslims believe that they are saved through making good choices that please Allah. During their life, they are never sure if they have done enough to make it to paradise. This means that many Muslims feel uncertain and worried about what will happen to them after they die.

Because of Jesus, a person can be sure they are forgiven, and confident they will be in Heaven. God wants Muslims to have that sure hope in Jesus. He wants them to know that through Jesus, there is nothing that could separate us from His love. As you read this verse, think about God's unbreakable love and the Muslim people who need to hear about it.

for i am
sure that neither
death nor life, nor angels no
rulers, nor things present nor
things to come, nor powers, nor height
nor depth, nor anything else in all creation,
will be able to separate us from the love of
god in christ jesus our lord.

-romans 8:38-39

THE CULTURE

Life in the Middle East is very different from America. Read about the Iraqi and Syrian lifestyles and imagine what it would be like to live in their culture.

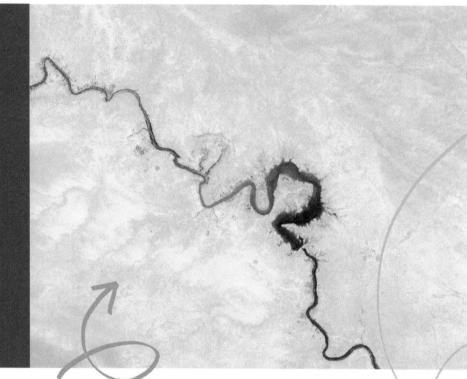

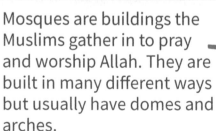

The Middle East is a large region that covers many countries. It's mostly hot, dry desert. If you're ever in the area, make sure you have plenty of sunscreen and water!

Mosques are buildings the Muslims gather in to pray and worship Allah. They are built in many different ways but usually have domes and arches.

Sometimes traveling across the desert can be dangerous. For hundreds of years people have relied on camels to carry them.

Many wars are being fought in the Middle East. Thousands of Iraqi and Syrian families are now living in refugee camps as they wait for a safe place to go.

In Islamic culture it is considered very immodest for a woman to show her hair. Sometimes women must cover their entire face, leaving only their eyes uncovered. It is only inside her own home with relatives that she is allowed to take her covering off.

SHARING
GOD'S STORY

How would you tell a Muslim person about Jesus?

Muslims believe it is very important to memorize the Quran. They work very hard to remember verses and stories perfectly. One way they remember the Quran is by putting the verses to music.

You can share stories about Jesus with Muslims through singing. Can you make up your own song using Scripture? Try to memorize the story of Jesus dying on the cross and God raising Him back to life.

Make the story into a song using instruments or even just your voice. Maybe you'll get the chance to sing your song to a Muslim friend!

In Islam, a song that is sung about the Quran is called "nasheed."

Hummus

ingredients

1 clove of garlic

1 can of chickpeas (drained)

1/3 cup of tahini (sesame paste)

3 tablespoons lemon juice

1/4 cup of water (or liquid from chickpea can)

1/4 cup of oil

directions

Step One:
Combine all ingredients in a food processor

Step Two:
Mix until smooth.

Step Three:
Transfer to a serving dish and serve with flat bread or veggies.

EAT LIKE
AN IRAQI

Many parts of Iraq are dry and not much can grow. But there is a place called the "fertile crescent." Many fruits, vegetables, and grains are able to grow here. Most of the usual Iraqi meals are made with ingredients from this region.

One food that is made in both Iraq and Syria is a dip made from garbanzo beans (some people also call them chickpeas). This dip is eaten with meat, rice, vegetables, and flat bread.

Want to give it a try? Follow the recipe above to see if you enjoy eating like the Iraqis.

PLAY LIKE A
SYRIAN

Children who live in refugee camps do not have the same opportunities that others do. Very few get the chance to go to school and get an education. Some don't have access to grocery stores or parks or even clean bathrooms. Children must be creative and resourceful as they find ways to have fun in these camps.

THE GAME OF HAJLA

YOU'LL NEED:
- 1 small rock
- 1 piece of chalk (or tape if playing inside)

GAME RULES:
Each player takes a turn to kick the rock while hopping around the grid on one foot. Starting at the bottom right corner and going counter-clockwise, the player pushes the rock to the second square with his foot.

The player continues through the grid as long as he does not hop on the lines or allow the rock to land on a line.

The seventh square with the X needs to be hopped through without any lines being touched and without the rock landing on any part of the X.

A player's turn ends when he either lands on a line, kicks the rock onto a line, or makes it through all eight squares without any mistakes. If no mistakes are made that player wins the round.

SETUP:
Draw eight squares on the ground using chalk. Or if you're playing inside then use tape on the floor. The grid should form a rectangle that is two squares wide and four squares long. The second to last square should have an X through it.

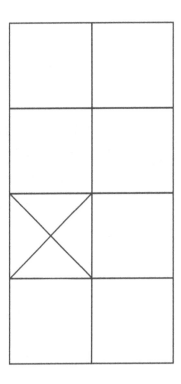

Want to give it a try? Follow the instructions above to play your own game of Hajla.

One Syrian game that children play in the camps is called Hajla. It's a little bit like American hopscotch, and it's an easy game to play in the camps because all you need is a small rock and a patch of dirt.

The game of Hajla has been played for many years by the children of Syria. The rules to the game are sometimes adjusted to include more children, or changed altogether depending on each group and how they want to play. Feel free to come up with your own unique rules as you play Hajla with some friends.

BUDDHIST

The last worldview we will look at is the *Buddhist* worldview. Use the animal symbols to help you decode the secret words. Then fit them into the correct sentences below:

Buddhists do not believe in _____. Buddha taught that everyone can save themselves by learning how to live well.

Buddhists believe that all of our sadness and _____ happens because we have _____.

If we can learn how to live rightly, we will be able to stop having desires and then we will not be sad or suffer anymore. This way of living is called the _____ _____.

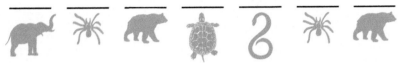

CODE KEY

DID YOU KNOW THAT EACH OF THESE ANIMALS CAN BE FOUND IN PLACES WHERE PEOPLE HAVE A BUDDHIST WORLDVIEW?

GENEROUS
JARS

MAKE A GENEROUS JAR AND HELP RAISE MONEY FOR THE PEOPLE OF MYANMAR!

Throughout this week we will learn about a particular group of people with a Buddhist worldview. They live in a country called Myanmar. You will watch a video about them, learn interesting things about their culture, and even try some of their food! As we learn about them, we will be raising money to help them. To get started we are going to create a generous jar. Here's how:

1   Grab your generous jar.

2   Fill out the word **BUDDHIST** next to the "B."

3   Begin filling your jar!

BUDDH

WHERE IN THE WORLD ARE

IST PEOPLE?

Myanmar   Cambodia   Thailand   Laos   Vietnam   Mongolia

DO CHRISTIANS AND BUDDHISTS HAVE THE SAME

WORLDVIEW?

Cut out each box on the dotted lines. Then read the sentence in each box. If it is something a Buddhist person believes, paste it into the Buddhist column. If it is something the Bible teaches, paste it into the Bible column.

BUDDHIST

BIBLE

The universe was never made. It has always existed and will always exist.

I can never learn enough or become perfect enough to save myself from suffering.

The reason there is sadness in the world is because sin has separated people from God.

I can learn enough and become perfect enough to save myself from suffering.

After I die I will live another life. If I was good I will live in a good place. If I was bad I will live in a bad place.

The reason there is sadness in the world is because people want things they can't have.

After I die I will live again. If I trusted in Jesus to save me from my sins, I will live in Heaven. If I didn't trust in Jesus, I will live in Hell.

God created the universe and everything in it.

BUDDHIST
BIBLE VERSE

Buddhists believe that all of the suffering on earth is because we have desires. If we never wanted anything, there would be no suffering. Life is about learning how to stop wanting things. This is very hard and can feel very hopeless to many Buddhists.

God wants Buddhist people to know that not all desires are bad. God gave us the desire to know Him. He made us to want things like friendship and love. God wants to use those desires to help us have a relationship with Him. As you color this page, pray that Buddhist people would learn how God can fill the desires of their hearts.

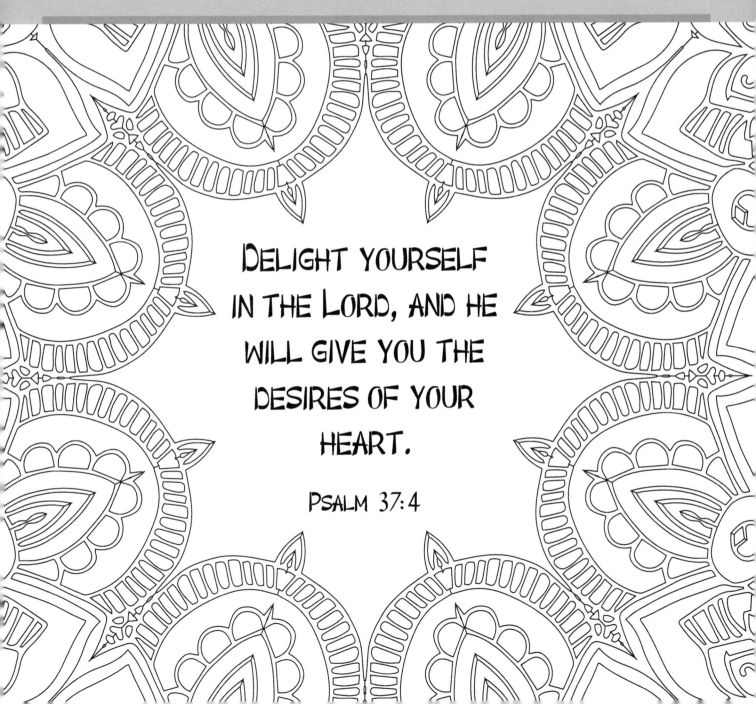

DELIGHT YOURSELF IN THE LORD, AND HE WILL GIVE YOU THE DESIRES OF YOUR HEART.

PSALM 37:4

THE
CULTURE

Have you ever thought about living in Myanmar? Read about the Burmese lifestyle and imagine what it would be like to live in their culture.

Myanmar is a country with many different landscapes. There are mountains, valleys, rivers, beaches, and even islands.

In Myanmar, people build temples called pagodas. The most famous pagoda is called the Shwedagon Pagoda.

Myanmar is a very religious place. Some people are Buddhist, others are superstitious. Many people pray to Buddha and offer incense in worship.

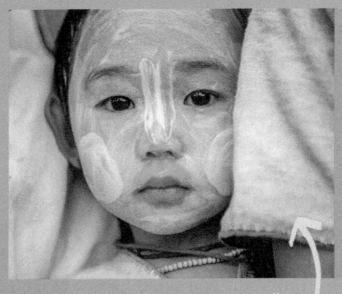

In Myanmar the sun can get really hot. Women paint their faces to protect their skin from the sun's rays and as a beauty treatment. This tradition is called thanakha.

Myanmar has many exotic animals. It has more tigers than almost anywhere in the world. People think some animals are lucky. If a person sees a white elephant in the wild they believe they will have good fortune.

SHARING
GOD'S STORY

How would you tell a Buddhist person about Jesus?

Did you know that you can teach a Buddhist about Jesus through dancing? In many Buddhist cultures people dance as a way of telling stories.

One story they might find interesting is the story of creation. Most Buddhists don't know where the world came from because Buddha didn't believe it was important.

Think about the story of creation found in Genesis. How could you show this story through a dance? If you meet a Buddhist you might not want to start dancing right there on the sidewalk, but you can still talk to him or her about how God created the world.

Think of the 7 days of creation. How would you show what happened on each day?

Kyauk Kyaw

ingredients

2 1/2 cups water
2 teaspoons agar-agar powder
1/2 cup sugar
1 cup coconut milk
A pinch of salt

directions

Step One:
In a medium saucepan, stir together water, sugar, agar-agar, and salt.

Step Two:
Allow to boil on medium heat until the sugar and agar-agar dissolve completely.

Step Three:
Add coconut milk and boil for one minute.

Step Four:
Turn down the heat and simmer for two more minutes until you can see coconut solids separated on a spoon.

Step Five:
Pour into a pan and allow to set fully at room temperature.

Step Six:
Once set, place in refrigerator for several hours to cool. Serve chilled.

EAT LIKE THE
PEOPLE OF MYANMAR

In Myanmar, people don't eat as much dessert as we do here in America. When they do eat dessert, it is usually made with tropical fruits that are easy to find. One of their favorite desserts is called Kyauk Kyaw. It is a bit like coconut jello.

Coconuts take almost a year before they are ready to be picked. They grow on tall trees that make them difficult to harvest. Many people use ladders attached to the tree, or a tall pruner pole to reach the fruit.

Want to give it a try? Follow the recipe above to see if you enjoy eating like the Burmese.

CREATE LIKE THE
BURMESE PEOPLE

In Myanmar people make many different kinds of jars, bowls, vases and boxes using wood and a special paint called lacquer.

Objects that are sealed with lacquer are called lacquerware.

Lacquer is a liquid that gets painted on the outside of the jars. It helps protect them from being damaged by things like food and water.

In Myanmar lacquer is made out of juice from the Thitsi tree and mixed with ash. Each jar is carefully painted with many different patterns. Many jars have lids with spiral tops for added decoration.

WANT TO GIVE IT A TRY?
Follow the instructions to make your own lacquerware

YOU'LL NEED:
• a paper mache box or bowl
• paints
• 2 paint brushes
• high gloss mod podge
• newspaper (or a surface for drying your box)

1

Choose a craft box and paint it with your own creative designs.

2

Choose a button or bead to create your topper. You can glue a couple together to create a larger topper.

3

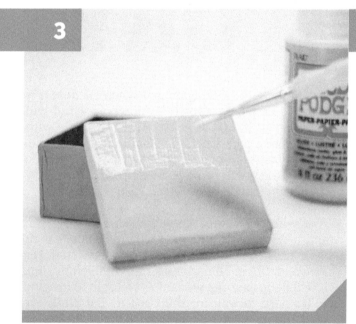

Once your paint is dry add your coat of mod podge. This is like lacquer and will help seal your box.

4

Once your mod podge dries, glue your topper on the lid and let it dry. Then use your lacquerwear however you'd like!

THE REST OF GOD'S STORY

Did you know that God's story didn't end with Jesus saving us from our sins? Of course, that is a very important part, but it's not the last part. Jesus is coming back!

He's coming to earth again and when He does it is going to be big! Everyone in the whole world will know about it. You see, Jesus won the battle with Satan a long time ago when He rose from the dead, but He hasn't announced His victory yet. When He returns there will be no mistaking who He is: He is the Champion. He is the Rescuer. He is Lord.

And when He comes, He will make a new Heaven and a new Earth without Satan. Without fear or weariness. Where no one can separate us from His love and where all our desires are fulfilled in Him. It will be so amazing we can't even begin to imagine it. It's hard to wait for that, isn't it? But while we wait, there are some people who might be interested in this story. Some who haven't heard it, or don't understand it, or might not believe it. What a very important job we have to tell them about Jesus!

CPSIA information can be obtained
at www.ICGtesting.com
Printed in the USA
LVOW05s1454091017
551752LV00023B/1427/P